DESIGN
YOUR
GARDEN

ID0954298

Published in Great Britain in 2008
by John Wiley & Sons Ltd

Copyright © 2008
John Wiley & Sons Ltd, The Atrium, Southern Gate,
Chichester, West Sussex PO19 8SQ, England
Telephone +44 (0)1243 779777

Email (for orders and customer service enquiries):
cs-books@wiley.co.uk
Visit our Home Page on www.wiley.com

All Rights Reserved. No part of this publication may be
reproduced, stored in a retrieval system or transmitted
in any form or by any means, electronic, mechanical,
photocopying, recording, scanning or otherwise, except
under the terms of the Copyright, Designs and Patents
Act 1988 or under the terms of a licence issued by the
Copyright Licensing Agency Ltd, 90 Tottenham Court
Road, London W1T 4LP, UK, without the permission in
writing of the Publisher. Requests to the Publisher
should be addressed to the Permissions Department,
John Wiley & Sons Ltd, The Atrium, Southern Gate,
Chichester, West Sussex PO19 8SQ, England,
or emailed to permreq@wiley.co.uk,
or faxed to +44 (0)1243 770620.

Designations used by companies to distinguish their
products are often claimed as trademarks. All brand
names and product names used in this book are trade
names, service marks, trademarks or registered
trademarks of their respective owners. The Publisher is
not associated with any product or vendor mentioned
in this book.

This publication is designed to provide accurate and
authoritative information in regard to the subject
matter covered. It is sold on the understanding that the
Publisher is not engaged in rendering professional
services. If professional advice or other expert assistance
is required, the services of a competent professional
should be sought.

Other Wiley Editorial Offices

John Wiley & Sons Inc., 111 River Street, Hoboken,
NJ 07030, USA

Jossey-Bass, 989 Market Street, San Francisco,
CA 94103-1741, USA

Wiley-VCH Verlag GmbH, Boschstr. 12,
D-69469 Weinheim, Germany

John Wiley & Sons Australia Ltd, 42 McDougall Street,
Milton, Queensland 4064, Australia

John Wiley & Sons (Asia) Pte Ltd, 2 Clementi Loop #02-01,
Jin Xing Distripark, Singapore 129809

John Wiley & Sons Canada Ltd, 5353 Dundas Street West,
Suite 400, Etobicoke, Ontario M9B 6H8, Canada

Wiley also publishes its books in a variety of electronic
formats. Some content that appears in print may not be
available in electronic books.

Executive Commissioning Editor: Helen Castle
Project Editor: Miriam Swift
Publishing Assistant: Calver Lezama

ISBN   978-0-470-51763-5

Cover photo © Steve Gorton

Cover design © Jeremy Tilston, The Oak Studio Limited

Photo credits
All photographs by Steve Gorton unless stated below:
p 26 © istockphoto.com/AtWaG,
pp 35 (t &b), 69 (t,c & b) © The Garden Trellis Company Ltd,
p 46 (b) © Mobilane (UK) Ltd, p 76 © Alan Wilson

Page design and layouts by
Jeremy Tilston, The Oak Studio Limited
Prepress by Artmedia Press Ltd • London
Printed and bound by Printer Trento, Italy

© Mixed Sources
Product group from well-managed
forests and other controlled sources
FSC   www.fsc.org Cert no. CQ-COC-000012
© 1996 Forest Stewardship Council

The paper used for this book has been independently
certified as having been sourced from well-managed
forests and recycled wood or fibre according to the rules
of the Forest Stewardship Council.
This book has been printed and bound in Italy by Printer
Trento S.r.l., an FSC certified company for printing books
on FSC mixed paper in compliance with the chain of
custody and on products labelling standards.

DESIGN YOUR GARDEN

Garden Style Guides

CAROLINE TILSTON

Photography by Steve Gorton

DESIGN YOUR GARDEN

INFORMATION

Introduction   6

1. What do you want?   14

2. Inspiration   24

3. Reality   30

4. Base plan   36

5. Design   42

6. Movement   50

7. Materials   56

8. Colour   64

9. Plants   70

10. Fun bits   76

11. Step by step   84

INSPIRATION

Introduction   90

1. Lines   92

2. Spaces   102

3. Pink   112

4. Seaside   122

5. Sculpture   132

6. Pinball   142

7. Surprise   152

8. White   162

9. Circle   172

10. Amphitheatre   182

Directory   192

Introduction

Changing your garden can be one of the most exciting things you can do with your home. The scope for change and the possibilities for improvement are endless. Unlike inside, in the garden you don't have to worry about what the space is for – it's not a kitchen or a bedroom – it's a space. A space for you.

Have fun

So whatever your taste, whatever your style, you can indulge yourself in your garden – you can let your imagination run riot and have fun. Inside the house you're much more constrained by practicalities but outside you can create spaces, make new rooms, indulge your fantasies … in short, go to town. And you can do this any way you like, you don't have to follow the rules or do sketches and scale drawings. Some of the most successful gardens I've ever been in have been laid out directly on the ground and created on the spot – no preamble, no plans. But it doesn't always come this easy.

Getting stuck

When people do get stuck with their gardens, the two things they often say are – 'I don't know where to start' or 'I've got so many ideas I can't decide'. This is where a little help, a defined way to get to a finished design, can come in handy.

Step by step

There is a logical process to designing gardens, a number of steps to go through. I haven't invented it – they teach it in garden design schools and it does work. What I have done is simplify it and, I think, boiled the whole thing down to its basics so it's even easier to pick up. The first four steps are all about gathering information, once you've got all that information it's easier to create a great plan. It's about combining what you need, with what you want, with what you've got. Once all that information is collected you make the spaces in the garden, construct it and decorate it. Sounds easy.

TIP

If you really do get stuck ask a garden designer to come and have a look at the garden for a couple of hours. Most designers offer this service and it can really help overcome specific problems and set you on your way.

Creating rooms

Later in the book I'll go on a lot about 'creating rooms' in the garden, it's a crucial point to getting a great design. When I teach garden design, before they start, people will often come up with something like this …

This is placing the elements where you want them; it's not going to give a strong design.

Take the same garden and think about creating nicely proportioned spaces and you start to get something like this …
You can still have the lawn, seat and flower beds where you wanted them but, because we've started by making nicely proportioned shapes that will feel good to be in, it will be a good strong design.

Or just enjoy the pictures …

In this book I've outlined 10 steps to get a great garden. Follow them and you should end up not only with a beautiful garden but also with one that works and does all you need it to. You don't have to go through the whole lot if you don't want to. It would be just as good to draw inspiration – look at the sketch plans in the book which fit the shape of your plot, or just find a beautiful garden and transpose it onto your site. I know measuring and drawing and doing things to scale puts a lot of people off – you don't have to do this if you don't want to, just skip the chapter, design on the ground, sitting in the garden. This is the way many of the best gardens in the world were laid out – with sticks and string in the open air.

Golden rules
- Have fun
- Keep it simple
- Don't fill the garden's area – create spaces within it.

The Ten Steps

Step 1 – What do you want?
This is all about what you need from your garden. Everybody needs slightly different things – but often it revolves around prosaic things like washing lines, sitting areas, planted areas.

Step 2 – Inspiration
Now this is where everyone is different – you might draw inspiration from a garden you've already seen, one in a picture, or even not from a garden at all. I once saw a garden inspired by an abstract painting. Inspiration can come from anywhere – clip and keep, take photographs, gather together a mood board of images.

Step 3 – Reality
Back down to earth – what is actually outside your back door right now? What's good, what's bad? What can be changed, what needs to stay the same? Mark these all down and bring them to the party.

Step 4 – Base plan
This is where I might lose you. If you can't cope with tape measures and scale drawings, don't worry, just pass this chapter by … design outside in the garden – no worries about getting the measurements right then.

Step 5 – Design
This step is where all the information about what you need, want and have got come together, and the important message here is that you're creating rooms, spaces within the garden. Concentrate on getting those spaces looking good and the garden will take shape.

Step 6 – Movement

Now you've got the perfect spaces marked out you need to work out how to move between them. How to get from the house to the garden, how to get around the garden and how to entice people to explore.

Step 7 – Materials

We've got a design now – but what to make it out of? Should the main space be of grass or of gravel? Should the divisions between the rooms be plants or trellis? This is the chapter to help you decide.

Step 8 – Colour

Colour comes from plants and from hard materials. How best to use colour in the garden and what effects you can get – this chapter runs through the colour basics.

Step 9 – Plants

Like Chapter 4, I might lose some people here, but what I aim to do is to look at plants as a product for the garden (sacrilege to plant lovers I know). So I'll go through some of the different functions of plants and list some that fulfil each function – it really helps to demystify the whole thing and, it's just what a lot of professional designers do.

Step 10 – Fun bits

And finally, this is all about decorating the rooms – choosing the perfect water feature or sculpture – shopping really.

What do you want?

Function is a great place to start with any design. What do you want from your garden? Do you want to sit in the sun? Do you need a place to hang your washing, a den for the children and adults?

The usual suspects

People's needs from a garden, by and large, tend to be quite similar, so it's possible to do a checklist that should at least in part be relevant to you. Every need will have an effect on the plan – so I've listed below not only the needs but also the likely upshots of those needs.

Need	Solution
Low maintenance	Many people put this high on their list of needs. You don't want to feel you have to go out there every week and do stuff if you don't want to. Four simple ways to keep the maintenance down … **1.** Lose the lawn – and more generally, the more 'hard' landscaping like paving that you have in the garden, and the fewer plants, the lower the maintenance will be. **2.** Where you do have plants put in evergreen structural plants that don't need a lot of attention – bamboos are the flavour of the moment. **3.** Designing the garden in itself will help to keep the maintenance down – the shapes will be stronger and more defined. That means a little neglect won't look too bad. **4.** Don't stress about it, maybe keep one area quite neat but call the rest a wildlife garden.
Seating area – for how many people?	**1.** The best place to start with this is to think of the table you want. A huge 10-seater table is going to need a different scale of seating area to an intimate table for two. **2.** Whatever its size, don't forget you need to get around the backs of the chairs when people are sitting in them. 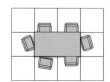

Seating area – in the sun or shade?	If at all possible look to see where the sun and where the shade is at different times of day and throughout the year. It's sometimes surprising where it will hit – a gap in houses may make one spot perfect for evening dining, or a tree might provide a perfect shady spot for summer lunches. It's often unrealistic to spend a year looking at the garden – if you're moving into a house ask the people you're buying it from, they will probably know.
A lawn (or not?)	If you want lawn you will need a storage place for a lawn mower. (See below for fors and againsts.)
Area for children	If you want a specific area for children and their toys here are some things to think about … **1.** Try to put in some shade so they don't get burnt in the sun. **2.** Have storage so their toys can be tucked away. **3.** If you're having a tall structure, like a climbing frame, think about putting it next to the house so it doesn't dominate the garden. **4.** You may not need a 'children's area' at all. Often expensive play frames are a five-minute wonder and sit unused and forlorn for years. It might be better to buy a small sandpit or put in a swing. Things that don't affect the overall garden design and can be got rid of if they're not pulling their weight.
Storage	There are loads of different shaped storage sheds on the market – the Internet is a great place to look. It's easy to size up what's available, what space you need and how much you want to spend and then mark it on the plan. One of the best places to put them is right against the house – so you can't see them when you look out of the window. Next to the house also means the storage is more secure and convenient.

Access around the garden

If you need to get down the garden all through the year you'll need a good, direct path. This may dictate the whole of the design, but don't ignore the need, if you have to get to a back gate twice a day nothing could be more annoying than having to take the 'scenic route'. If you do want a very direct path, put it on the plan first and design around it – but remember a path doesn't have to be one solid line, it could be stepping stones across grass, or part of a wider paved area.

Parking

1. Before you start it's a great idea to actually drive your cars onto the plot and see where the turning circles are and how much room you need to park. Make sure you can get out of the doors and around the cars easily if there's room.
2. Don't put anything in the way (like a flower bed) that's going to make life more difficult or get run over.
3. Three and a half metres is ideal for the width of a driveway.

Area for rubbish/ compost

This will be driven by practicalities – getting the bins out to the street, getting the rubbish to the bins; is there an ideal, easy-to-access-throughout-the-year place? As for compost, it shouldn't smell too bad, but best not to put it right next to the kitchen or sitting area, just in case.

Irrigation system

This is fairly easy to put on the plan, the leaky hose systems are the easiest to install and they will just snake around the base of the planting. You will need an outside tap though and that may need to be installed.

Greenhouse

If this is for bringing on cuttings it will need to get plenty of spring sunshine, so make a note of where that might be. It would also be good if it was near the outside tap.

Changing light …

You'll need to know where the sunny and shady areas of the garden are – knowing where north is will help but there's nothing like looking to see where the last rays of the sun hit, or where there's a sheltered sunny spot on a winter's day. In high summer at midday it doesn't really matter which way your garden faces as the sun will be pretty much directly overhead – it's at the margins where it matters. Early and late in the year a small north-facing garden may not get much direct light at all. If you want morning and evening sun, again you'll need a clear skyline to the west and east.

Gazebo/ summer house	These tend to be quite pretty so it's a good idea to put them in view of the house, and check that they're in the sun, if that's what you want. Also stand in the place they may be and look back, is there a good view, something for the eye to settle on?
An area for planting	Even if you want a low-maintenance garden you may want an area to potter in – to change from year to year. Two ways to do this – have a dedicated flower bed, or use containers. The containers will take a bit more looking after and more watering but you can hide them away if the planting isn't going too well.

For and against lawns

Good things about lawns

1. They give year-round greenery, a really important factor if your house is surrounded by buildings.
2. Compared to other types of plants, lawns are on the whole low maintenance.
3. They are cheap to put in and they can cover a large area. Grass seed in particular is very inexpensive although turf (rolls of grass you can buy like carpet tiles) is slightly more expensive.
4. Grass is great to lie on and children love to play on the lawn in the summer – it's hard to practise handstands on decking.

Bad things about lawns

1. In dry summers they bake and go brown; in wet winters they become impassable. If you need to get across the lawn all through the year you will probably need a path.
2. Lawns suffer lots of wear and tear, especially in a small area – lots of use will wear the grass away.
3. Small gardens tend to have very shady patches and lawns never do very well in deep shade.
4. Children can't ride bikes on a lawn or play in soggy winter weather.
5. Lawns are pretty much a wildlife desert – other types of planting or allowing the grass to grow up and flower will attract many more insects and birds.
6. Compared to decking or stone, lawns are pretty high maintenance.
7. You will need a lawn mower and somewhere to store it.

There are more reasons not to have a lawn than to have one – but, the arguments for having one may be more compelling than anything against. The cost of alternatives may mean that lawn is the only option, and if you have children there is something very special about having a lawn for them to play on. I think if you have a tiny garden, say under five metres square, a lawn becomes a bit unreasonable. You'll have more space storing the bits and bobs to go with it than you will have actual lawn. Also at that size the cost of paving is less of an issue.

Inspiration

T his is where the fun begins. What do you want your garden to feel like? It can be anything … perhaps a mini-Versailles, a water garden, a place to play pool outside, a sunken Jacuzzi.

Imagination

This is what's really changing in gardens right now. What was until recently pie in the sky, the sort of thing you only saw on some way-out television programme, is now achievable in many back gardens. Those fancy stainless-steel sculptures that, only a few years ago, came bespoke for thousands, are now available off the shelf for hundreds. The same is true for lighting and water features.

Lighting ...
Don't forget lighting – it can transform a garden. Even if lighting is beyond the budget at the start, put ducting in while you're digging up the garden, so it's easy to thread the cables through later.

Looking at gardens

Taking a single image or a single theme can really help to give direction to the garden. If you see a picture or a garden you really like, don't be put off because it's nothing like your garden. Think about the elements that make it appealing to you. It might be a path winding off out of sight, or bright, light paving or a contrast of strong lines and fluffy planting. Broken down to the basest elements it's often possible to transfer inspiration from the most unlikely of places.

How to avoid a themed garden

Creating a themed garden can look silly. A Moroccan garden, for example, with all its vibrant colours, transposed into duller northern light looks out of place, but adding touches, a light found on holiday or some tiles on the walls, will give a flavour without creating a pastiche.

Heaven

Up until very recently only the very rich have been able to shape their gardens to create their ideal landscapes, their heavens and havens on earth; but now, and really only in the last few years, people are coming around to the idea that anyone can do it. In any outside plot you can create your heaven – but how do you decide what your ideal garden is …

One garden designer asks – what was your garden like when you were growing up? What was your first memory of a garden as a child? Another designer asks – if you could have any garden in the world what would it look like?

Neat or not?

One dichotomy that I always like to get to the bottom of – are you a neat freak or a messy soul? Do you power clean your patio or do you think the weeds growing between the stones are romantic? It's little things like this that can alter the whole look of a garden and give really strong clues to what you'll like.

Neat freaks	Sloppy Joes
Mowing edges round lawns.	Plants drooping onto lawn and leaving petals.
Clean, power-washed paving. Make sure joints aren't recessed so no dirt can lodge between the paving stones.	Recess the joints, better still just butt the pavers up so there's lots of soil and weeds can colonise.
Use circles and straight lines to make the garden.	Experiment with curves and different angles.

Reality

Enough of the dreaming – back to reality. What have you actually got outside the door? And can that reality ever be squared with all those wants and needs? It pays to take a really careful look at what's out there already and think about what you like and don't like about it. Being specific can help to direct the design and narrow down what you need to do.

The plot

The reality bit is what designers call a site survey and site analysis, but, without the jargon, what you're doing is looking to see what's in the garden already, what's good, what's bad. What needs to be covered up, chopped down, made better. This is what designers call 'losing the plot'.

Like the 'needs' section, anything we list is going to have implications for the design so I've put down some of the likely elements of the garden and their ramifications.

What | So …

3

What	So …
What do you like about the garden as it is now? Maybe a blossom tree or a shady hideaway?	If you like something it would be good to keep it and make more of it. A lovely tree might need a lot of room around it or a contrasting coloured shrub nearby, for example.
What don't you like about the garden?	It might be that it looks awful in winter, is dull, or is too shady. Each of these will have an implication for the design and the planting.
Is there a great view that needs to be seen or an awful view that needs to be hidden?	If there's an awful view, you may want to put up a barrier so you can't see it. If there's a good view, you may want to put in a seat so you can appreciate it more.
Are you overlooked?	Tall screening may create privacy – wander around the garden to see where the most private areas are and whether anything would help, and how high would it have to be to screen you off?
Where is the sun – in the morning, in the evening etc.?	If you want your breakfast outside it might be good to put in a sitting area which catches the morning sun, or maybe a couple of seats to catch the last rays of the evening sun.
Is the garden exposed?	You may need to create a windbreak with trellis and hedges.
Too small?	If the garden's too small there's not a lot you can do, but there are some tricks that can make it appear bigger. (See below 'Trickery'.)

33

Boundaries that are ugly?	Ugly walls or fences can be painted, covered in trellis or battens, or hidden behind plants.
Structures that can't be removed and aren't pretty?	You need to mark these on the plan and incorporate them into the new design. Sometimes carbuncles are so big that trying to disguise them will only make them more obvious, but often a physical screen will work wonderfully well.
Structures that can be moved or removed altogether?	If you want to get rid of them and can, then don't even bother measuring these.
Manhole covers?	You can hide these in plantingor under paving (with a lift-off tray). Try to avoid having a lawn over them – they stand out like a sore thumb; and if you want to run a hedge line across one, there will be a break.
Boggy or very dry areas?	These may have implications for what you can plant. Grass, for example, will do badly in a boggy area or in a very dry area.

You can see that already some elements of the design are beginning to take shape – out of sheer necessity.

It may become clear now what the backbones of the design might be. If, for example, you want a large sitting area in the sun and there's only one place that gets the sun – well that's the sitting area.

Overlay onto this the feel you want, say a modern garden, so you think about straight lines and simple planting and layout, and you almost have a design.

Trickery

It's worth thinking now about a few elements which will make the garden seem larger.

1. **False perspective** Any element which emphasises the effect of distance will do this.
   - Using larger paving blocks or gravel nearer to the house and smaller paving blocks or gravel further away.
   - Making paths narrower as they move away.
   - Using slightly smaller versions of apparently the same decoration as they get further away from you – like stone balls, or columns.
2. **Covering up boundaries** If the boundaries of the garden can't be seen, the size (or lack of size) is less apparent.
3. **If the boundaries can't be covered** Use the same materials for the floor and the walls to give a larger expanse.
4. **Dividing the garden up** If you can divide the garden up it will appear larger, even if it's just to create a little hidden room at the rear which can be glimpsed from the rest of the garden.
5. **Mirrors** Will help to fool the eye into thinking there's more to the garden – always cover up the edges of the mirror with planting or with trellis to help the illusion along.

How do you make another 'room' for your garden even when there is no room? In this garden, above, an archway has been used to create the feeling of entering a whole new space – even if the space is just large enough for a seat. And below, a substantial 'doorway' has been created from trellis work, this time with a mirror behind it. Do it with conviction and these are great tricks to make a garden seem larger. All of the woodwork here is from The Garden Trellis Company.

Base plan

This is the final step in the process of information gathering – gathering measurements from the garden. This is the bit that can put people off – just skip the chapter if the idea of measuring seems like too much hard work. It is perfectly possible to work out a design on the ground, never touching a pen and paper.

Won't measure — can't measure

You don't have to do a base plan – it's very possible to go straight from Step 3 to design on the ground, and until very recently, that's how gardens were designed. When I worked in a huge National Trust garden, my old head gardener used to tell me about standing in for a statue when he was a boy so the grand landscape garden where he worked could be designed in situ.

If you lack small boys, get spray paint from a builders' merchant and draw direct onto the ground to make the shapes. A stick and a length of string will help form a circle. The same string between two sticks will give you a straight line (you can see why designers are so keen on straight lines and circles – laying out the garden is a doddle).

Start measuring

However, if you want to get an accurate drawing and assess the real shape of the plot, it might be time to get the tape measure out (it's actually easier if you have two tape measures).

> **TIP**
> Life gets really complicated if you mix imperial and metric measurements.

If you have a standard-shaped rear garden, measuring up isn't that difficult …

1. Measure right across the garden, along the back boundary, and then right down the garden.

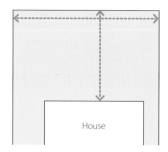

2. Measure across the back of the house and note how much space there is at either side of the house (if any).

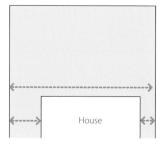

There, that was easy … The complications come if you have an unusual shape to the garden or you have lots of things in the garden you want to keep and so have to put on the plan. The idea is that you put the house down on the paper first and then relate everything to the back of the house.

Here goes …

1. If you do have an irregular shape or if you want to keep things that are there already, the way I find easiest is to run a tape measure right down the garden from a fixed point on the house, say the left-hand side of the back door, and make a note of where anything crops up. So you'll then know that the apple tree is 6m away from the house.

2. Then measure how far the apple tree is from your line and you can find its exact spot in relation to the house.

3. For something like a shed you get a couple of measurements in the same way and then measure up how big the shed is to plot it.

4. If your garden is a funny shape this method will work to plot its shape. So, for example, if at 4m out from the house the fence is 5m away from your line, and as you go further from the house the fence gets further away from your line – so at 6m away from the house, the fence is 8m away – you can then transpose this onto a plan to get the direction the fence is taking.

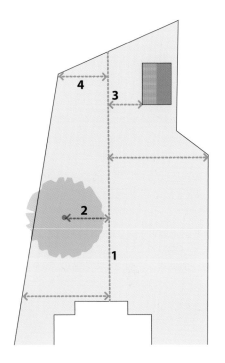

Google it …

Don't forget Google Earth – if your plot is big you can get a really good idea of its overall shape from Google Earth. Or … look out of an upstairs window to help get an idea of its proportions.

Drawing up the plan

The next thing to do is to transfer the measurements onto paper. The easiest way is to use 1cm on the paper to represent 1m on the ground; this is 1:100 scale. If you want your finished plan to be bigger on the paper use 2cm on the paper to represent 1m on the ground (1:50 scale).

Some useful symbols for you to use
These are at 1:50 scale. So a bench which is 1.5m long will appear 3cm long on the paper.

TIP
Squared or graph paper makes drawing up easier.

TIP
It's not necessary to get the plan accurate to the last centimetre – especially if you're using a contractor, they will always take their own measurements anyway.

A useful grid
This grid is 1:50. Each box represents 1m on the ground. So if your garden is 7 metres long count off 7 boxes.

4

Scale 1:50
1 Metre

Design

So you know what you've got, you know what you want, you know what you need. Now it all needs to get onto that plan. If you're designing on site, now is the time to use line paint and string to mark out rooms and pathways through the garden. If you have something on paper, now is the time to start sketching out your master plan.

Start designing

Once you've got a plan with everything on it that can't be removed, make lots of photocopies and start to sketch things out. Go back to your original list of needs – putting these onto the plan, to scale, will give you a good start, but at this stage think in terms of broad areas rather than specific shapes. So you have a seating area somewhere back there, a children's area over to the right, a patio next to the house.

Rooms

This is really key to good garden design. Remember you're making areas within the garden – you are making rooms. Rooms with good proportions, that feel good to be in. Rather than being hidebound by the overall shape of the garden, you're trying to make these rooms not too cramped, not too open. A long thin garden, for example, needs to be divided into better proportioned spaces – that are not too long for the width.

Why create rooms?

1. Dividing the space makes it seem bigger (really it does).
2. The rooms, the spaces you make, can be of nicer proportions than the original shape of the plot.
3. Making rooms creates surprise and makes hidden corners.
4. Those divisions will also help to give privacy.
5. By making divisions like this you will help to hide the boundaries of the garden so the size, or lack of it, isn't apparent.
6. The rooms you make, like rooms in the house, can have different functions and this helps to make sense of the garden and the design.
7. All these divisions and entrances will help to frame views and create vistas. Often a vista is formed right down the garden – helping to emphasise its length without having to live with a long narrow space.
8. All these divisions are great at hiding things you don't want to be seen like a shed or septic tank.
9. But most of all they will give you a good strong design.

How to divide?

There need to be divides to make the rooms – but how to make these and what height should they be? They don't have to be very tall, even a low wall will make an 'implied division' which is enough to give the impression of different areas. High or low, the usual way to make divisions is with …

1. Trellis or fences
2. Planting
3. Walls
4. Hedging

Make the lawn a good strong shape …

One of the great ways to define a space or 'room' in a garden is with the lawn. This is one of the great secrets of garden design and it applies to loads of gardens – make the lawn a good strong shape and you're halfway to designing a garden. Fill in what's left with beds and a sitting area or whatever is needed and, hey presto, a design.

These panels of climbers come ready grown from a company called Mobilane and provide instant, green dividers.

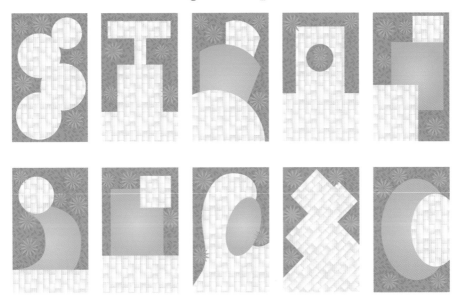

Getting the proportions right

John Brookes, one of the founders of modern British garden design, invented a system for setting out the rooms and deciding the proportions of them in the garden. He uses the size of a dominant feature of the house to create a grid across the garden and then uses this grid to make spaces and infill. For example, he may use the width of the major window overlooking the garden and repeat this as a grid over the whole area of the garden – some of the grid's squares will be paving, some grass, some planting. As he says, '... the grid will encourage you to unfold your design from your living space instead of relating it to the boundaries, the downfall of many garden designs'.

TIP

There is a design school in London that won't let its students use anything but straight lines and circles. It sounds draconian, but they know that it's a pretty sure way to get great designs. Simple strong lines and shapes make powerful designs.

Add on the needs and wants

This is when to bring in all those wants and needs that made up the design brief; it all starts to come together …

- A washing line in a sunny spot, not too far away from the washing machine and with some hard-standing access so you can get to it in soggy spring weather.
- A play area for the children, maybe tucked away behind one of those divides you've incorporated to make the garden rooms.
- A shed – again if you've used rooms or even just put a really strong shape on the lawn, you should have created lots of spaces around the lawn for sheds, sitting areas and hideaways.
- A patio for evening dining.

Make sure the patio is big enough ...

Patios are usually made too small. One way to get a good size is to use the same size as the back of the house. Too big? Maybe it would fill up your garden and half the neighbours' too. Another way is to put your table and chairs out there. Pull the chairs out as though people were sitting on them and then you need to be able to walk around the back of the chairs ... Now that should be big enough.

So, you've got your areas or rooms, how do you get around them?

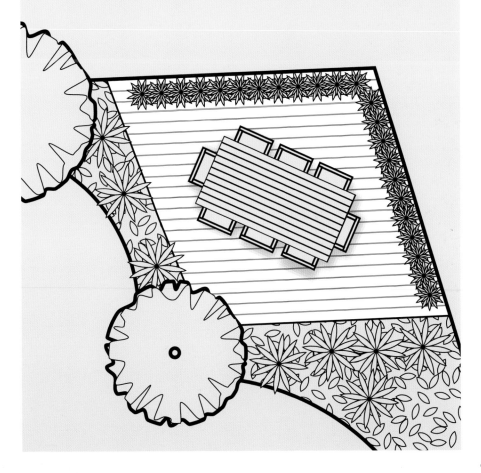

Movement

This is an area that's often not mentioned but it's hugely important. Even in the tiniest space there's an important question of movement – between house and garden, and around the garden.

A journey

While you're out there measuring up or pondering possibilities, think about how you're going to get around the new design. Is there going to be a journey through the garden – how will it begin, what is the entrance like, will there be any surprises?

From a more practical point of view, do you need to get to the bottom of the garden right through the year – can you do that?

Paths

My old head gardener used to say you should always be able to have two people walking side by side down a path, even if they have to hold hands. Narrower than this and it's a bit antisocial. One metre across or above is ideal.

Trickery
Paths that get narrower as they go away from you will look longer. Paths that zigzag through the space will make the journey longer and the garden seem larger.

Lines of desire

This is the way people want to go –
usually the most direct route from A to B,
and being lazy folk, that's the way most
of us will go. When you're designing, you
can either go with these lines and put
paths in where the desire is, or you can
fight it and make it so difficult to go in
the straight line that it becomes easier for
people to go your way. So, for example, if
you put in some big shrubs across the
line of desire, it's easier to go around
them than through the dense planting
and you can then direct people to where
you want them to go. Why would you
want people to go other ways than the
most direct route? So that they make
that journey around the garden, and to
show off all the corners of the garden.

Ways to direct movement around the garden

6

1. From the terrace or patio –
   surround the terrace with plants
   and create a space in the beds to
   make a real entrance. These
   planted areas will also help to
   nestle the patio into the garden.
2. Use focal points – something that
   stands out like a statue or a water
   feature to catch the eye and guide
   people out to take a closer look.
3. Arches and tunnels are even
   better at enticing; people can't
   help but take a look to see what's
   down there.
4. Obviously paths will take people
   on their journey.

When the land rises up from the back of the house

This is a situation that comes up again and again. If your garden is on a slope you get this problem of trying to make usable spaces, especially next to the house. If your garden is on a slope and you put an extension on the back of your property you have a real problem – extending the house outward creates a steep drop down to the extension and you might be looking out at a bare retaining wall near to the house; and, with your new extension, with all of those windows or patio doors, it is hugely important what this view is – it needs to look good and you need to be able to get out to the garden easily through your new doors.

But if you push the patio back into the garden you make that retaining wall larger and the further you push it, the larger that wall becomes.

The answer? The only satisfactory answer I've ever seen is to bite the bullet, push the earth back, build retaining walls around three sides and decide how to get up to the other part of the garden. This will almost inevitably mean steps.

Here the wall has been curved around the lawn and the steps put to each side – curving around to invite you into the garden.

This slope wasn't too marked. A low retaining wall around a large seating area provides extra seating and helps with the feeling of enclosure.

When the drop to the back of the house is large you can step the retaining wall and make terraced beds. The planting then softens the impact of the drop. These slick, rendered walls give a good contrast to the soft planting contained within them and the steps are off to the side, away from the entrance so you aren't looking out of your extension up a flight of steps.

Another way to help with a drop is to have the steps rise up and round, so the retaining wall you see from the house is only half the height of the drop.

Or you can use the retaining walls to hold wonderful features and planting, and then hide the steps to one side.

Movement between the house and garden

Most of the time you're stuck with how this works – a back door, a side return, a French window if you're lucky; but, when it comes to putting an extension on the back of the house, all of a sudden you can completely change the way your garden and house work together. It's a wonderful opportunity to rethink the whole feeling of house and garden and, in general, the more open and accessible one is to the other, the better. This is what they call blurring the boundaries between inside and out. Huge windows can bring the outside in, doors and French windows can take the inside out.

- Having the same floor height between inside and out makes it really feel like it's one space, but take advice on this – solid flooring needs to be two bricks below the damp-proof course of the house.
- Using a similar design inside and out helps to reinforce this flow, the feeling of inside and outside being one space.
- Using similar materials on the floor is, in theory, a great idea to reinforce this feeling, but many materials weather more and change colour outside much more than inside so the two only look the same for a year or so.

Materials

Now you've got the areas and your paths and access ways, you need to decide what's on the ground and what's making the divisions. There are plenty of choices to be made, don't assume that the big area front and centre has to be lawn – what if it's gravel? In a small garden you might want to dispense with the lawn altogether.

Floor

The choice of floor materials is absolutely enormous and it is really difficult to tell what will look good all over the patio when you've only got one or two of the pavers or slabs to look at – it's like choosing a paint colour from a tiny swatch. The best thing to do is to go to a builders' merchant or DIY shop that has large displays or show gardens. Even better, if you ever see something in a garden which you like the look of, ask the owner what it is.

> **TIP**
> ....
> Wet the material so you can see what it looks like in the rain, some get better, some get worse.

Questions questions

Michael Heap of CED Ltd has been dealing with natural stone, especially paving and aggregates, for over 30 years. He's learnt a thing or two about its selection and suggests that the place to start is first to ask yourself a few questions about what you want from the stone *before* you start to choose the type or colour.

1. **How modern, slick and clean do you need your paving to look?**
   Or is it country cottage style? If the garden you're planning is very modern and clean-looking, don't go for a porous material like sandstone unless you're prepared to clean it often. A less porous material like Italian porphyry,

quartzite, granite, or slate might be a better bet – the dirt and water won't seep in and it will stay looking fresh without much input.

2. **Or do you want an old-world, reclaimed look?** Nothing quite beats used York stone slabs for this, but as well as being quite expensive they are also thick – so you'll need a good depth to lay them in. Take care too if the reclaimed slabs have a cleaned, sandblasted surface, it may be to hide oil or dryness. If there's oil in the slabs it will start to come out again in sunshine. If the slabs have spent their life indoors they may be so dry they are crumbling away.

3. **Will there be cars or just people using the stone?** If laid well, many materials used as flags or setts can take the weight of cars and even lorries. Correct preparation of the base is critical. It does add to the cost, but is definitely worthwhile. Two options – either make the concrete base, the bedding mortar and the stone so well bonded that they act as one, or go for a flexible construction and lay smaller units (like setts) on a fine crushed aggregate bed on a compacted sub-base. Whichever method, seek some technical advice.

4. **Do you want dark colours or light?** Designers go for greys, garden-owners go for warmer colours. If you want a really light colour, try granite or Jura limestone, but darker colours (and multicoloured stones) do show the dirt less.

5. **How much do you want to spend?** Indian sandstone is very reasonably priced and might look like the right answer just on that ground alone, but remember that it is porous (though not always as porous as York stone) so will absorb water and, therefore, dirt and will look much darker a few years down the line. Also inexpensive is gravel. It is one of those things that divide the world – the gravel-lovers and the gravel-haters, although there is a compromise. Often it's better to lay some good quality stone with gravel around it than to lay a cheap and relatively poor paving stone everywhere.

6. **Once you've thought about these questions, seek advice to help you achieve the result you want.** There are so many natural stone possibilities, it is a fascinating subject.

Other things to think about …

The decisions don't end when you've chosen the paving. Also think about …

1. **Which way is it going to be laid?**
   I have a confession here. We got our kitchen done last year and had large slate slabs laid. I came home from work and they were going lengthways down the kitchen. I hadn't specified which way to lay them – but I had wanted them laid crossways to make the space look wider, my fault but I could have cried.

2. **The pattern** Random and complicated will look more cottagey and more old-fashioned. Slick and simple will look more modern.

3. **The mortar** This is where the whole thing can fall apart. Light, wide mortar can dominate any stone and spoil the whole effect. Go for a mortar that's near to the same colour as the stone (it can be dyed) and not too wide. If you have it recessed, it will look better but will catch dirt and then weeds. A favourite of mine is to have the materials butt-jointed with no visible mortar. For old-fashioned styles and patterns this looks lovely and natural. For modern materials and layouts it looks slick.

4. **The cut of the material** Sawn will have a smooth, slick, modern look; riven will be more natural with texture in the surface.

5. **Environment** Indian sandstone is cheap because it relies on cheap labour – there are sources available that guarantee fair wages.

> **TIP**
> At design colleges they teach you to find out the price of hard landscaping by taking the price of the paving and then times it by three to get a rough total price for the job (labour being twice the cost of materials). It's not always accurate but it's a sobering guideline.

Decking

Decking has had such a bad press lately that there is probably a real backlash against it, but it really does have a place in the garden, especially if the ground is uneven and you want to make a sitting area.

How to get decking to work

1. Use it where it's appropriate – to make a raised platform or to create a flat area on uneven or sloping ground. Decking can look wonderful if used to make platforms at different levels. One of the most appropriate places is over water or a boardwalk next to water.

2. Bed it into the garden, plant around the back of it and around the front – create entrances to the decked area. Make a space between the decking and wall, or fence behind it, to get some plants in to break up the surfaces.

3. Use treated timber planks rather than decking boards if you want a more natural-looking effect, though they will be more slippery in wet weather.

Boundaries & walls

The overwhelming message about boundaries in small gardens is – unify or hide!

Unify

It would look odd to have a room inside the house with different things covering each wall but this is the situation in many back gardens. One wall made of old fencing, one of brick wall, one of new fencing. Unifying the walls will make the whole garden feel better.

1. Paint, or, even better, render and paint.
2. Trellis or wooden battens hung over the boundaries will work wonders.
3. A formal layout of plants can help to give meaning to the different walls – say topiaried bay trees set two metres apart all around.

Of these three, rendered walls are definitely the thing right now in gardens. As well as on the boundaries, they can be used inside the garden.

1. They make great surfaces for shadows, so they go well with planting which either catches the sun or is lit at night.
2. They are perfect to form into shapes which hold water features and in-built seating.
3. Most of all they have smooth and sleek modern lines which fit perfectly with modern interiors.

Capping

Capping (or coping) is what the top of a wall is finished with to stop water getting inside it. If you put brick, tile or stone capping on a rendered wall it will veer towards the Mediterranean, cottagey look. Stick with very sleek capping to keep it modern (sawn stone or stainless steel), or even no capping at all.

Colour

C olour in the garden. The main colours in the garden will come either from plants or from hard surfaces. Colour from plants will be much more ephemeral and change with the seasons. Anything like paint colour is there for good and will show up much more in winter.

Colour theory

I'm always sceptical of people writing about colour – most of it is opinion or fluff – what can you say? Some colours look nice together and some don't? Well that's all a matter of opinion. Then there's the endless reams of gushing stuff that's written about the emotions of colour – well that's up to you. What I want to know is what will actually help when it comes to choosing the paint colours or picking the plants?

- A colour wheel can help to give guidance. Colours next to each other on the wheel will combine harmoniously, colours opposite each other will give contrasts – the ones directly opposite will give the dazzling contrasts.

- Using cool and hot colour themes can help. Hot colours like reds, yellows and oranges will give a definite look to the garden and work well in sunny spots. Cooler colours, like white, purple and blue, often look good in shady areas. White, especially, glows at twilight in shady spots.

- But don't feel you have to stick to either of these if you see something that breaks the rules – sometimes it's great just to go around the garden centre and put some flower colours together and see what happens. If you do it this way you're pretty certain to get the flowers coming at the same time in the future.

- Yellow deserves a special mention. Many, many people dislike it – why? It doesn't react well with blues or many reds, and it can seem too strident without any of the sexiness of deep purples and reds … in short, I have no idea why people don't like it, but if you don't, you are not alone.

- Dark purple is a really useful colour in the garden and sets off many other colours dramatically. Things like smoke bushes or a red-leaved cherry can be mixed with lime greens for a really zingy effect. Reds also work well with dark purple, so do greys and so do dark blues. It's a very useful place to start to build up a colour composition.

- Another tip, which may help, is to remember that, generally, the overwhelming colour in the garden is green and green can make the most wonderful backdrop to just one or two other colours. Some of the best gardens in the world are green gardens. It's a bit like a black and white photograph – all of a sudden you're relying more on shape, line and texture, and shadow.

Colour wheel

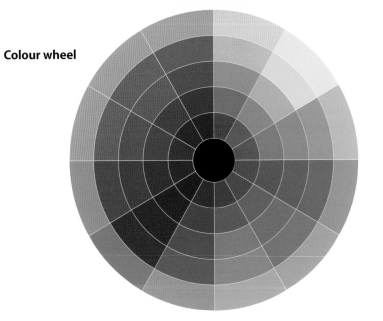

8

Putting different colours together can give some exciting combinations …

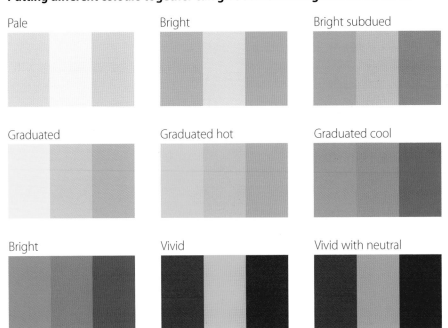

Pale

Bright

Bright subdued

Graduated

Graduated hot

Graduated cool

Bright

Vivid

Vivid with neutral

Hard surfaces

- You can paint your garden in the same way as you paint a room inside the house, but the difference is the huge variation in light through the day and throughout the year. It's worth taking this into account – a white wall that gets the full glare of the summer sun might be unbearable, but a wall which struggles to get any light at all will benefit hugely from being painted a light colour.

- Be careful with very bright colours – they look great in sunny climates where the light is strong, but can look overbearing and out of place in our climate. Muted colours are a safer bet.

- The boundaries are the most likely places to get colour from paint in the garden. A single flat colour, especially a light or bright colour, will visually jump forward and can make the garden seem smaller. Darker colours and colour washes will give a more camouflaged effect and help the boundaries recede.

- The main thing is to have fun with colour and try things out.

Q&A

Julian Furness of the Garden Trellis Company has been installing and painting trellis for over 15 years.
Here are some tips for using colour on trellis and other hard surfaces.

1. Simpler colour schemes work best, maybe just using one or two colours in the whole garden.
2. Trellis can form a frame for the garden, to set off the plants and the design. It works best if the frame is not too jarring.
3. Pastel colours work best – they can add interest but then you allow the plants to do the shouting.
4. If you do want to use zingy colours think how they will look in winter. A bright yellow wall may look fine with all the colour in the garden in summer, but in winter it might look isolated.
5. When you pick a paint colour consider how natural light changes through the day. Painting a section of wood and looking at that outside can help to choose colours.
6. Paint it before it goes up. If possible spray it – you need quite a bit of space but you can hire spray guns and it will be a lot easier than with a paintbrush.

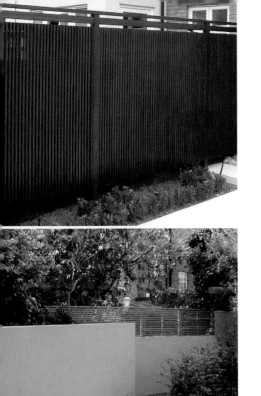

TIPS

White will jump forwards especially at dusk, use darker colours to blend back.

A stain will allow the natural wood to show through, paint will make a flat colour. If you use stain, the natural variations in the pattern of wood will help to blend it into the background rather than a flat colour of paint, which will tend to jump forwards.

Colours with grey in them will look much more natural. Even bright colours with grey in them will have an earthy quality which will stop them zinging about.

New trellis soaks up a lot of paint so put a coat of cheaper undercoat on first.

These trellis from The Garden Trellis Company show the benefit of working with toned down colours.

9

Plants

This is the bit that people can get really scared by, but don't be put off. There's a lot to be said for just having a go – get some plants, put them in and see what happens – funnily enough that's just what the 'experts' do to build up their knowledge.

There are great resources now to help you. On www.crocus.co.uk you can specify just what you need under their 'plant search' section. A tall plant for a shady spot that's evergreen and up will come a few suggestions. But there's nothing like going to the garden centre and falling in love with something.

TIP

If you want flowers and interest through the year, go down to your garden centre once a month and buy something that's looking good. Do this through the year and you'll have a garden with year-round appeal.

Another tip is to …

Plant it in the middle of winter – so you know you've got some structure. Then fill in the pretties which will look good at other times of the year during the year.

Glossary

Herbaceous perennial or perennial
A plant which is around all through the summer, dies each winter (either leaving nothing above ground or just dead stems), but does come back up again next year.

Annual A plant that grows up and dies in a single year. So it won't be around next year (unless its seeds have sown themselves).

Plant Directory

Here's a simple guide to get you started. I've grouped the plants by their *use*, which is a great place to start when you're planting up a garden.

Evergreen

1. **Lily turf** Green grass-like plant that flowers in autumn
2. **Leather leaf sedge** Taller grass-like plant with red/gold leaves
3. **Star jasmine** Climber with white scented flowers in summer
4. **Shrubby veronica** Blue summer flowers and pinkish leaves
5. **Fountain bamboo** A bamboo with more leaves than stems.

Architectural

1. **New Zealand flax** Strappy leaves from a single point
2. **Japanese aralia** Large, flat leaves on a tall shrub
3. **Hosta** Perennials with large oval leaves
4. **Spurge** Tall plant with zingy green flowers in spring
5. **Fountain bamboo** Has height, movement and shape.

Plants that look good on their own — used en masse

1. **Tufted hair grass** Airy flowers on golden stems
2. **Bamboo** Great to make tunnels or archways
3. **Giant feather grass** At over five feet tall this can provide screening through the summer
4. **New Zealand flax** Can look brilliant if used over a large area
5. **Hebe** - Evergreen and making a good mounded shape.

Low-maintenance plants

1. **Smoke bush** A shrub with great red/purple leaves
2. **Mexican orange blossom** Evergreen bush, with white scented flowers
3. **Christmas box** Smaller, evergreen and with scented flowers in winter
4. **Japanese anemone** If they're happy these will grow themselves with pink or white flowers in late summer
5. **Black lily turf** Black grass-like leaves, this is slow growing and slow spreading.

Plants for a really shady corner

1. **Lily of the valley bush** Spiky leaves and yellow flowers, it will survive almost anywhere
2. **Elder** Try the black-leaved elder for a more exotic look
3. **Lady's mantle** This can survive in a tiny bit of soil in a shady courtyard
4. **Lily turf** This evergreen plant will be happy in a shady place
5. **Lungwort** With flowers in late winter it's a good plant to put somewhere it can be seen from the house.

Plants that don't need watering

1. **Pheasant's tail grass** A really soft-looking quite small grass
2. **Lavender** Evergreen, scented and good during droughts
3. **Montbretia** Bright red or orange flowers come after spiky leaves later in the season
4. **African blue lily** Has purple or white flowers late in the season
5. **Rosemary** Evergreen with great scent and purple flowers in spring.

Plants for winter interest

1. **Hellebore** With wonderful shades of purple and pink these flower right in the middle of winter
2. **Pheasant's tail grass** The gold and red of the leaves come in autumn and stay throughout winter
3. **Black lily turf** Low-growing and evergreen, plant lots of it to make a black carpet
4. **Winter honeysuckle** This is a tall shrub and not very pretty but the winter flowers make up for it with a great scent
5. **Christmas box** The flowers on these small evergreen bushes will make a whole garden smell great in the depths of winter.

Fast growers

1. **Elder** I've seen this put on five feet in a year; choose the black-leaved one rather than the green, which is more of a weed
2. **Mexican orange blossom** Once it's happy this will shoot away and fill a difficult spot
3. **Geraniums** From one or two plants you can fill a whole area by dividing them every autumn into threes
4. **Fennel** This shoots up to five feet and more in a single season
5. **Clematis montana** This is a perfect climber for a large area, even if it's shady it will grow strongly and produce white flowers in spring.

It's interesting to see which plants come up in different categories. Bamboo is the most useful and you could do a lot worse than use just bamboo in the garden. I've seen plenty of amazing gardens that do just that.

Fun bits

The final layer in the garden is often the most fun to do – these are the decorative elements which add character to the ensemble. Although they come last they will work best if they are part of the design – a specific space in the design for a water feature or a sculpture will help it to feel part of the garden and not just plonked on top.

This beautiful stainless-steel water feature is by Alan Wilson.

Lighting

There are two types of lighting in the garden. It's easy to forget that sunlight is a wonderful light source. Think about the shadows of a tree's branches on the lawn, of reflections in water, of plants outlined against a crisp wall.

Natural light

Natural light changes through the day and it's worth thinking about how it moves and how to make the most of it. Low morning sun or late evening sun look amazing coming through diaphanous planting. A drop of winter sunshine should have a seat to catch it – and if the seat is out of any cold winds you could have a lovely place to make the most of the outside on a cold winter's day.

Making the most of dark areas in the garden

1. Use reflective surfaces – steel, water, light colours, anything that will bounce light around.
2. Paint the walls. Brick walls especially suck up light, so just painting them will have a huge effect. If you render them first the surface will be smoother and give back even more light.
3. Light materials on the ground will throw up more light.
4. Light-feeling plants – no heavy dark green plants on walls, use bright light-coloured plants like white bleeding hearts and Japanese anemones.
5. Put in artificial lights – kind of obvious but even in the middle of the day these can be useful to lift an area, and after dark, well, these dark areas come into their own, they are no longer disadvantaged.

Artificial lights

Functional

If there are any steps, paths, ponds or access ways – these will need to be lit so people don't trip. There are also motion sensor lights to help deter burglars – traditionally, until a few years ago, these functional fittings have been what garden lighting was all about.

Decorative

But beyond this functional role, garden lighting has a huge part to play in making gardens exciting and fun. I know people say that evenings are rarely warm enough to sit out and enjoy those lights – but think of the view you get from the sitting room window, lighting can make a magical scene and that can be enjoyed all year round.

Buying lights

Lighting is now big business on the Internet, everything from cheap and cheerful spots and fairy lights to serious bits of art. I've put some addresses below that I've found helpful in the past.

Lighting designer

If you're serious about lighting do think about getting a lighting designer in – they can give some wonderful ideas which will lift even a modest garden into the realms of art.

Lighting effects

- Backlighting

- Mirroring

- Underwater lighting

- Uplighting

- Floodlighting

- Grazing

- Spotlighting.

Web addresses

www.lightingforgardens.com
www.lightingsensations.co.uk
www.rawgarden.co.uk

Water features

Five tips

- It sounds obvious but you need a place for your water feature. It might be central to an area, hidden in the planting or up on a wall. This will help narrow down the choice.
- Most water features will need power but not a water source, you may need to top it up occasionally but that's all.
- You might want to make a decision early on between modern or traditional. Modern, stainless-steel water features can be more flexible – obviously they look good in a contemporary garden but they also, by creating a contrast, look good in more traditional gardens.
- Do you want still or moving water? Still pools or ponds will create reflections but a fall of water will make a noise and, if placed correctly, will catch the light.
- Off the shelf or bespoke? This choice will probably come down to cost, but if you want something different it's worth exploring how a one-off water feature can be built. Many websites now will supply all the elements to make your own water feature.

Sculpture and ornament

Hide it or put it up front?

It's a lot easier to get sculpture to look good if it's nestled amongst the flowers and is something you stumble across. If you put it front and centre you have to be more sure that it's going to hold the area, that its proportions are going to be right, that it's going to look like it belongs rather than ludicrous. Ah, the potential for mistakes is huge.

TIP

If you're putting it as a central piece make a similar shape out of cardboard and live with that for a while, so you can catch the shape out of the corner of your eye and study it to see if it fits.

Five tips

- Challenge the sense of scale – a huge piece against the wall of a tiny garden will work well, as will stumbling across something that looks immense and half buried.
- Have fun, it's possible to make your own sculpture and ornament out of wood or marine ply then paint it.
- Light it – so at night you can enjoy it too.
- One at a time – if you have more than one sculpture on view it will begin to look like a gallery.
- Surprise is always going to be a winner. If you put the expected country urn in a country garden or a stainless-steel water feature in a modern courtyard it will be fitting but not interesting.

Furniture

Four tips

- Cheap is cheerful, it might fall to bits more quickly but a great advantage is that it tends to be lighter and easier to move around than the expensive stuff.
- Built-in seating has huge advantages:
  - You don't have to store it, it's always there and available.
  - It reinforces the structure of the garden rather than cluttering it up.
  - In a small space you can get many more bottoms on seats.
  - Disadvantage – the expense of having it built.
- I think we should have more really comfortable things outside – roll the sofa outside – but of course they will have to be moved back when the inevitable rain and frosts come.
- Surrounding a seating area with plants has lots of advantages:
  - It makes you feel more secure when you're sitting there – you're not out on a limb.
  - You can see and smell the plants as you sit.
  - If you're surrounded by plants the area will feel like an escape.
  - If the plants are tall enough they can give privacy to the area.
  - Scented flowers are great but be careful of those that attract wasps.

Step by step guide to getting the garden right

O nce you've got your plan and you know what you want to do with the garden – what next?

The ideal time to do all of this?

- The only season-dependent thing in the whole of this list is right at the end – the planting.
- You shouldn't plant when the ground is frozen solid, and you want to plant at a time when there is some rainfall – young plants need water at least until they get a little established.
- For big projects I think it's best to plant in October so you know there's the best chance of them getting a good foothold before they may get baked the following summer.
- The second best time is early spring and hope it's not too dry.
- If the garden is small enough that you can provide the water – by hosepipe, leaky hose or whatever – then you can pretty much plant any time during the year.
- But, for most gardens, the trick is to end up at point 7, the planting, in October.

1. Planning

Check you're not breaching any planning regulations. It's always worth a phone call especially if you're in a conservation area. Taking out trees, putting in fences or structures near to boundaries all may need permission.

2. DIY or not?

Decide whether you want to do the work yourself or get a contractor in to do it, or do *some* of the work yourself. Unless you are very keen on DIY it's usually a good idea to get help with walls and patios.

(Just by-the-by, if you are going to use contractors it might be worth phoning them at this stage to get a site visit booked for step 6 time, especially in the spring, they can be busy for weeks ahead.)

3. Clearance

Clear the garden of everything that's not necessary to the new design. You may need a skip for this and access becomes a vital ingredient. If everything has to be taken through the house or through narrow alleys it will all take a lot longer. Try to make access as easy as possible.

4. Marking out

Go out into the garden with the plan and a tape measure and mark all the areas on the ground using spray paint from a builders' merchant. String and pegs are very useful, both for marking straight lines and for creating circles (you can see why designers prefer these shapes to irregular swirls and curves – it makes life much easier). Spray out the shape of the lawn, the size of the patio, where the paths are going to be. Take a really good look at this and live with it for a while … and change the design if it's not working.

5. Hard materials

You pretty much always do the hard landscaping first – the bricks, patio, walls. Although it's possible to dig up the soil and to prepare the beds at this stage they may get trampled on, and it is now that all the areas of hard landscaping should be finally decided on so you can either get a contractor in to quote or, if you're doing the hard landscaping yourself, measure up the areas and put the order in for the materials.

TIP
Make sure, where the lawn meets the paving, the grass is higher so you can run your mower right across the edge of the grass.

6. Contractors

Once you've decided on a contractor, book them in as soon as possible and try to get a firm start date and an idea of how long the work will last.

Tips for getting the best out of contractors

1. Ask for the quote to be broken down so you can see where the money is going.

2. Get a start date and a finish date. This is one of the biggest causes of falling out between clients and contractors. With the best will in the world, contractors get too booked up or behind because of the weather and they may be unavoidably delayed getting to you – try to factor this in; but something you shouldn't put up with is a contractor leaving your garden halfway through to go to another job, so specify that this shouldn't happen and get a finish date.

3. You need to ask lots of questions about materials, jointing, finishing off, and ask to see samples of everything. The more communication you have with the contractor, the more likely it is that they will understand fully what you want and you will understand what they intend to do.

4. If anything doesn't look right – shout immediately; don't assume that it will come right in the end.

5. Check that they guarantee the standard of their work – the best way to get a contractor is through personal recommendation.

6. Make sure the main contractor is responsible for any subcontracted labour.

7. And finally, make sure there's something in the contract about leaving the site in good order at the end of the job and removing all rubbish ('arisings' is the technical term) from the site.

7. Planting

As the hard landscaping takes shape you can be more certain about the sizes and shapes of borders for plants and it's possible to work out a plan for them. I think it's easiest to do this on site, especially for a small garden. It might take a couple of trips to the garden centre but it's by far the most straightforward way. Get some of the plants you want in and put them on the beds with enough space around them to grow into the site. Re-arrange them if necessary so they look good and only plant them once you're happy with the layout.

TIP

Even the most experienced of gardeners and garden designers rarely get the planting right first time. With planting it's always an ongoing thing and at first there are bound to be some holes, some things doing too well, some things dying.

Inspiration

If you're designing your garden, looking at other designs is invaluable – to get specific ideas, to get a feel of what you want and also how to use materials.

If you like something you see, but think it won't fit in your garden, try to analyse the reason you like it. Break it down in this way and the elements become more transferable to your garden. For example, if you like a shady avenue but haven't got room, think about what it is about it you like. The repeated pattern of upright stems (you can do this with a pergola in a smaller space)? The patterns of the branches on the grass (easy to replicate in most gardens)? Or the shady feel to the avenue (again, quite easy to put into your design)? Or, then again, it might be the three acres of ground around the avenue that you like – that I can't help you with …

Lines

I

Sometimes garden design passes over into the realm of art – the fusion of materials and plants, the proportions, the clean lines, the sheer, perfect simplicity of it all. The design here is deceptively simple – a straight path leads straight down the garden. To either side are blocks of planting, water or hard landscaping. What makes it work so well are the perfect proportions and the immaculate detailing.

The owner of this garden wanted a serene sanctuary and by keeping the lines simple that's exactly what Ann Pearce, the garden's designer, has achieved.

This perfection still rests on those first principles of dividing up the space and making rooms. Ann has used the sloping site to create three level changes that span the full width of the garden, each one appearing to 'float' over the one beneath. Two paths slice through the horizontal bands, each one passing over the canal and through the meadow planting to create separate areas within the garden.

This simple division of space gives the garden a great feeling of calm, a feeling enhanced by the limited choice of plants. There are no fountains to disturb the water; just a perfect reflecting pool. There are no curves or diagonals in the plan. This gives a stillness to the composition, where everything is settled and balanced. A perfect tranquil haven, not only for the owner, but for all the wildlife that now shares the space with him.

The finish and attention to detail is impeccable. But despite the formality of the design, there's a softness and a wildness about it, the fluidity of the grasses and the rustling of the trees acting as a wonderful counterbalance to the strong lines of the house and garden.

Garden Plan

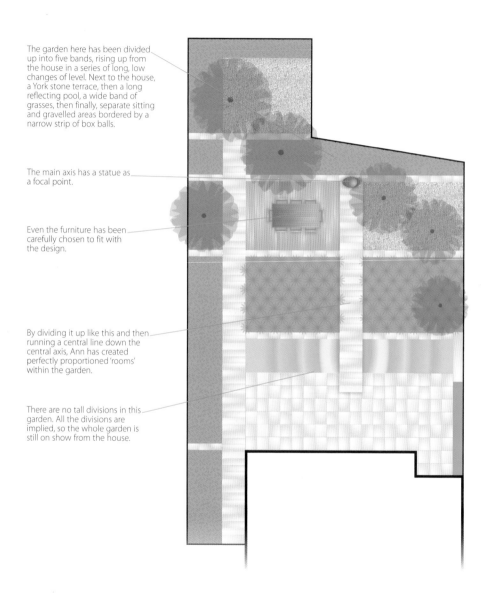

The garden here has been divided up into five bands, rising up from the house in a series of long, low changes of level. Next to the house, a York stone terrace, then a long reflecting pool, a wide band of grasses, then finally, separate sitting and gravelled areas bordered by a narrow strip of box balls.

The main axis has a statue as a focal point.

Even the furniture has been carefully chosen to fit with the design.

By dividing it up like this and then running a central line down the central axis, Ann has created perfectly proportioned 'rooms' within the garden.

There are no tall divisions in this garden. All the divisions are implied, so the whole garden is still on show from the house.

▶ A cloud-clipped elm tree mirrors the image of the box balls and makes great shadows on the walls.

◀ By overhanging the stone treads and copings, a narrow band of shadow is created, so that they appear to float, as if weightless, above the lower level.

▲ The sawn York stone creates the most wonderful sleek lines at the edge of the deck and the bridge across the pool.

▲ At the end of the central axis is a Buddha's head.

▼ To one side is a minimalist composition – a simple stainless-steel and iroko bench, a multi-stemmed tree and gravel bounded by a York stone border and box balls.

▲ Other than the trees, there are no tall uprights within the garden.

▼ For much of the year this garden is entirely green and gets its interest from shape, form and shadows.

▶ Box balls like this can, if planted together, make a wonderful, sculptural cloud-like effect.

Spaces

This is a textbook example of how to design a back garden.

The overall shape of the garden, with its bare fences, is incredibly awkward and to get a garden to work has meant creating beautiful spaces *within* the boundaries of the area. In the new design those fences in no way dictate the shapes of the new garden rooms.

Before

Ian Smith, from the design company Acres Wild, has created a garden formed of interlocking rooms each of which is a pleasure to be in. Freeing yourself from the lines of the boundaries is an incredibly important lesson in garden design and this layout shows exactly what can be achieved if you do.

The new rooms are surrounded by deep borders of lush planting – planting which hides and disguises those boundary fences, provides shelter from neighbours and leads the eye to the widest part of the garden.

But as well as solving these great practical issues, Ian has also addressed one of the most difficult points of garden design – creating interest and surprise. The garden rooms help on both these counts – it's easier to be interested and surprised if you can't see the whole garden at once. He has also added unusual touches and one of the really exciting elements to the garden is the deck surrounded by water at the sitting room entrance. Decking always looks good next to water and this is a great way to bring excitement to the garden and to the view out from the house. The stepping stones over the water to reach the garden are a brilliant way to lead you and your eye in this direction, into the main part of the garden and away from the nearby fence to the other side.

Garden Plan

The owners of this garden wanted to be reminded of their favourite holidays in Thailand and Malaysia, so the planting is tropically lush and green.

Further away the garden opens up more, with a wide green lawn to give the impression of openness and space.

All the boundaries have been clothed in greenery so the space is no longer dominated by the fences.

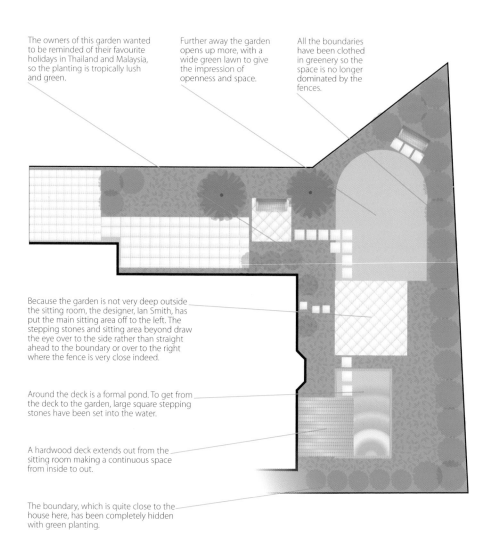

Because the garden is not very deep outside the sitting room, the designer, Ian Smith, has put the main sitting area off to the left. The stepping stones and sitting area beyond draw the eye over to the side rather than straight ahead to the boundary or over to the right where the fence is very close indeed.

Around the deck is a formal pond. To get from the deck to the garden, large square stepping stones have been set into the water.

A hardwood deck extends out from the sitting room making a continuous space from inside to out.

The boundary, which is quite close to the house here, has been completely hidden with green planting.

▶ Stepping stones through the planting echo the stepping stones around the pool – instead of water between the stones, there are pebbles.

▲ The stepping stone theme has been used again in the slabs in front of this bench. Rather than grass growing around the stones, mind-your-own-business – a low-growing, small-leafed plant – has been used.

◀ This place has been specially chosen because it catches the evening sun; it's the perfect G&T spot. To make this room feel more separate, a different pattern of paving has been used on the floor and the entrance is marked by a line of pebbles.

▶ The beds are dressed with pebbles to stop weeds coming through and to cover any bare earth. This is a lovely golden grass for a shady spot (grasses usually do best in the sun) called Hakonechloa.

◀ A wide bed around the house is filled with large clumps of tropical-style plants.

▲ This is the hugely important view from the sitting room. The boards run at right angles to the property to help give depth to the deck, and heavy planting disguises just how close the boundary is to the house here.

▼ A water spout keeps the water moving and provides interest.

Pink

This beautifully designed garden is all about creating spaces which work with the house. The owners have a wonderfully modern kitchen with huge windows overlooking the lower garden. The space they now look out on is a seamless continuation of that modern pink interior. Upstairs, the inside decoration is more traditional and the garden reflects this change.

So Stuart Craine who designed the garden has created two very distinct spaces here. The lower level is full of twinkle and bright colours but then, reached by a staircase, the space at the higher level is more restrained, a more traditional garden.

The lower level is designed to fit with a recently built, light and bright extension. This outdoor space, confined by retaining walls, forms a continuation of the new room. When the doors are opened the whole area becomes one space.

At the upper level the garden forms the main view out from the older parts of the house. A more restrained and traditional garden was called for. But the areas are not completely unrelated – both use the same sandstone paving and the same clipped hedges, to give continuity to the whole space.

The two areas do have a very different feel and to separate the two Stuart has used the level change to enhance the feeling of entering a new place. As you rise up the steps and turn a corner you are very aware of the change in mood. The turn in the steps was done for practical reasons, to fit a large number of steps into a small area, but Stuart has turned this to an advantage by creating a surprise that unfolds as you turn the corner.

Planting in both areas has been kept to a minimum and the maintenance has been kept down further by using only one type of plant in each bed.

Garden Plan

The upper area of the garden is formed into a dining area bordered by small trees.

This view from the kitchen is incredibly important in the garden and much of the designer's work has been to disguise the steep rise up from the patio and make the most of the walls around it. This garden could be dominated by ugly walls; as it is, the walls have been turned into the most wonderful feature of the garden.

Steps rise in two flights up to the higher level.

This garden fits perfectly with the interior of the house – modern and funky, even the pink has been carried through from the interior.

The doors of the sitting room can be pushed right back making inside and outside one enormous space, so it was important that the two areas, inside and out, formed one design.

▶ The pink is interesting – at first glance it's very bright and zingy, but it does have a lot of grey in it to give it a chalky appearance. This grey tones the colour down and makes it more acceptable.

◀ The side wall of the garden is rendered and painted a bright pink. If left on its own this huge wall would overpower the garden, but its impact is lessened by the climbing plants and the large metal planter.

▲ The sawn-edged sandstone forms a smooth and slick capping stone for the pink wall.

▼ When you see the view out of the ground floor window, above the kitchen with the pink sofa, you realise why the designer has made the upper level of the garden so traditional – it fits beautifully with the restful, classic-style room from which it is seen.

▼ Blue LED spots set into the pink wall lead the way up the stairs.

▲ The doors to the kitchen fold right back so the inside and outside blend as one space.

◀ Pleached trees, trees which form a hedge on stilts, have been used to enclose the sitting area at the higher level.

▶ The shimmering wall water feature is made from sheets of gold leaf applied to a base. It shimmers rather than shines and adds a stunning yet subtle wall of metal to the lower area.

Seaside

This garden is all about taking inspiration from your surroundings and working with what you've got – however inhospitable the environment might seem. The original layout and concept was by garden designer Debbie Jolley although over the years, as the garden has been implemented, the owners have added much of their own with found objects and places for children to play.

Here on the Sussex coast there is very little soil, the ground is covered with shingle and stones, tall things don't grow naturally this close to the beach and the landscape is open and flat. The temptation is to either fight against nature to try and create a typical English country garden, or to give up and let nature take hold. But this garden shows how to work with the environment using what's there to create something beautiful, in harmony with its surroundings.

There are loads of great ideas here, especially if you're drawn to a seaside theme. This place is full of things which fit with the seaside and they've been put in the garden in a natural way. Found objects are placed in such a way that they could have come in as flotsam and jetsam. Upright wooden planks echo the groynes along the seashore; a boat looks as if it may have been washed up with the tide.

From a pure design point of view it is interesting to look at how the garden is divided. There are no tall divisions or verticals in this garden, all the divisions are implied – but it works; the different areas and the structure are clear.

Garden Plan

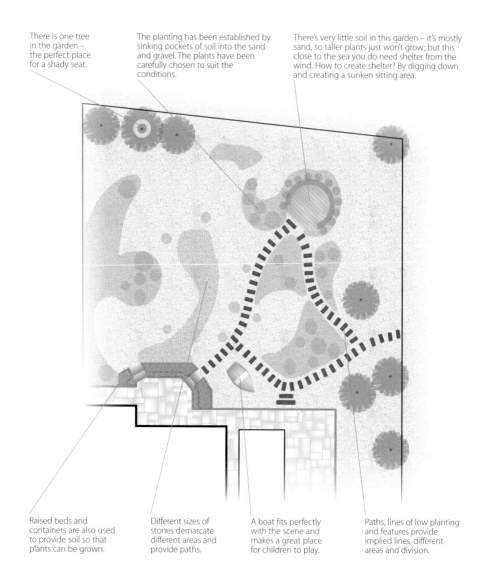

There is one tree in the garden – the perfect place for a shady seat.

The planting has been established by sinking pockets of soil into the sand and gravel. The plants have been carefully chosen to suit the conditions.

There's very little soil in this garden – it's mostly sand, so taller plants just won't grow; but this close to the sea you do need shelter from the wind. How to create shelter? By digging down and creating a sunken sitting area.

Raised beds and containers are also used to provide soil so that plants can be grown.

Different sizes of stones demarcate different areas and provide paths.

A boat fits perfectly with the scene and makes a great place for children to play.

Paths, lines of low planting and features provide implied lines, different areas and division.

▶ Upright sleepers make a retaining wall totally in keeping with the garden, leading you down to a sunken area. Painting them and cutting them to different lengths makes them more decorative and less forbidding.

▲ In this windy environment the below-ground area is the perfect place for sitting.

▶ Where there are plants, the sand and gravel had to be dug out and a pocket of good soil put in.

▲ The lining of the pond is hidden by large boulders.

◀ Wooden planks with a centre of cobbles make a great decoration in the centre of the sunken area. This effect could be used in any gravel area.

4

▲ Sedums are great for this type of environment – they can survive in very little soil and through periods of low rainfall.

▲ Over the years the owners have accrued many things, picked up from walks on the beach.

▲ Larger stones are used to guide you through the garden and mark different areas.

◄ Tucked away near the house is a raised playhouse for children.

▼ At the centre of the garden is a pond surrounded by wooden posts. To make the pond look more natural, the surrounds have been dug out so there are slopes down to it and it sits lower than the surrounding garden.

Sculpture

When you're designing a garden it's often difficult to imagine what it will look like in a few years' time. When you put in that little shrub that hardly reaches your knee it's hard to think that in a few years it will tower over you, but plants do grow and it's worth looking at this garden to see what a mature design looks like. After several years the garden has a lived-in look – it looks comfortable with itself, but the layout still follows those golden rules of creating spaces within the garden.

The main space is formed by the lawn, the second space is a hidden leafy area beyond. By dividing it up like this the designer, George Carter, has made a long garden into two manageable, well-proportioned areas.

The rear area is an exciting shady realm with a grotto and hidden seats which makes a great foil to the open stately lawn area near the house.

But what makes this garden unique is the way it has been decorated. George is a master in the use of ornament. In the lawn area a single tall urn, rising out of the foliage and bright against the green, sets the tone for the whole garden.

The other ornaments in the garden follow its lead. Even though the area isn't large they give it an air of opulence and well-being. The folly hidden at the rear, the huge planters and the statues in the front of the house, all give a character to the garden. Without these ornaments the garden would be aimless and unstable, with them it has personality.

Garden Plan

Right at the back of the garden is a folly.

This area beyond the lawn is completely hidden from view, you reach it through an arch and passageway. The arch is wonderful – narrow with no hint of what lies beyond, you can't help but be drawn to explore. A path that curves out of sight is a wonderful way to get people to explore the garden and to hide the size of it.

An urn hidden amongst the foliage gives a focal point and an air of grandeur to the garden – a great example of decoration lending character to a space.

The planting all around the lawn is evergreen, so the garden looks this good all through the year.

The lawn forms the main 'room' of this garden.

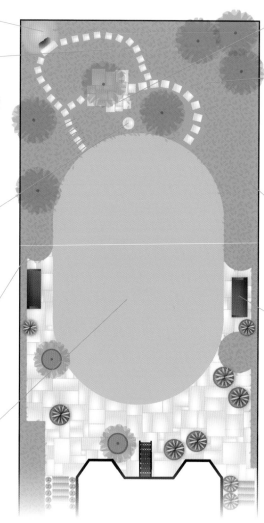

A shady sitting area is hidden amongst the greenery.

The garden is long and quite narrow. George Carter, the designer, has cordoned off the rear of it to create two areas, two rooms with good proportions. The first room holds the lawn, the second room is full of surprises.

Not one inch of the boundary can be seen in this garden. The borders are deep enough to accommodate the large shrubs which totally enclose the spaces.

Seats have been placed at each side of the garden, set on York stone to match the terrace; they are a further invitation out into the wide lawn space.

▶ Behind the arch the planting is romantic, jungly and overgrown.

▲ The terrace, created from random-laid York stone, is full of found objects and decorative pieces.

▲ At either side of the steps up from the cellar George has put a line of containers.

▲ And the most wonderful surprise, a folly. Clad in concrete set with stones and shells, it makes the perfect focal point for this shady rear area.

◀ Large lead containers fill the terrace and old-fashioned watering cans provide an interesting display.

▼ Ferns and other shade-lovers have been used to make the most of this enclosed rear area.

▲ Benches nestle in the planting but they are placed on a stone platform so they don't sink into the soil.

▶ A pathway leading off through an arch to somewhere secret – a perfect enticement to carry on.

▼ Throughout the garden these huge pots, each holding a large olive tree, decorate the garden but aren't too fussy.

▼ At the rear of the garden, hidden away in the shady spot, is a fernery with a hidden seating area.

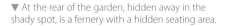

Pinball

The family who live here had very particular needs from their garden. The children needed somewhere to play, the family wanted to make the most of the sunny, south-facing terrace on the back of the house and they wanted something that looked good all year round but was understated. The part of the brief which has resulted in one of the most interesting elements of the garden was the need to satisfy the clients' 'delight and obsession with plants'. The owner wanted a garden where he could study and grow a wide range of them.

There are a lot of ways to do this. One of the most obvious would be to build different glasshouses and have different beds within the garden. That would work but would completely take over this town garden. Ian Kitson, the designer of the garden, came up with an ingenious solution to create the effect on a smaller, more manageable scale. He has used bespoke planters, each with a different microclimate and soil to suit different types of plants. These he has put next to the house where they act like a parterre – a semi-formal start to the garden, designed to be viewed from the house above.

Rather than have a regular pattern, Ian has used organic shapes for the planters. They could have been oblongs or squares and arranged, as you might expect in a town garden, in a geometric pattern, but the layout he's used is easier on the eye, more interesting, and it gives all the structure you would get from a formal garden without the constraints of a regular layout. For example, if this had been laid out more traditionally, all the beds would have had to be the same size, not sized to suit the plants, and you would have a limited number of ways through to the rest of the garden. This less formal design offers more ways through and is much more inviting. The layout has also given a memorable name to the garden – the pinball garden.

Garden Plan

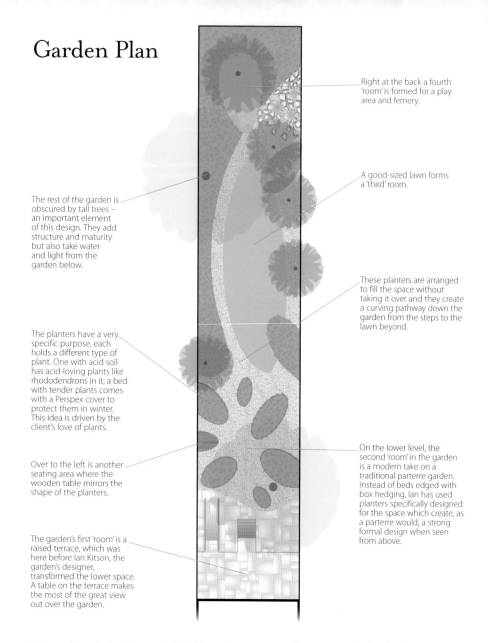

Right at the back a fourth 'room' is formed for a play area and fernery.

A good-sized lawn forms a 'third' room.

The rest of the garden is obscured by tall trees – an important element of this design. They add structure and maturity but also take water and light from the garden below.

These planters are arranged to fill the space without taking it over and they create a curving pathway down the garden from the steps to the lawn beyond.

The planters have a very specific purpose, each holds a different type of plant. One with acid soil has acid-loving plants like rhododendrons in it; a bed with tender plants comes with a Perspex cover to protect them in winter. This idea is driven by the client's love of plants.

Over to the left is another seating area where the wooden table mirrors the shape of the planters.

On the lower level, the second 'room' in the garden is a modern take on a traditional parterre garden. Instead of beds edged with box hedging, Ian has used planters specifically designed for the space which create, as a parterre would, a strong formal design when seen from above.

The garden's first 'room' is a raised terrace, which was here before Ian Kitson, the garden's designer, transformed the lower space. A table on the terrace makes the most of the great view out over the garden.

▶ Beyond the planters, the garden's third 'room' is a green area of lawn surrounded by shrubs and ferns. The path's trajectory is set by the organic layout of the planters – it follows the same curve, this time around the unstructured shape of the lawn.

◀ There are different types of plants in each container – Mediterranean, prairie, meadow, acid soil lovers, plants which love damp soil, and cacti and other desert planting. This cacti planter has its own Perspex cover to protect it from the winter wet.

▲ The planters come together like a loose formation of petals to form an organic pattern on the ground.

▼ The children's playthings are well hidden at the back of the garden and are essentially dispensable to the design. In a few years' time when the children have outgrown these, the garden will look none the worse for their removal.

▼ The designer has extended the existing York stone terrace out into the garden to form a sinuous edge rather than a traditional straight line. This builds on what is already in the garden but introduces the principal theme, the main shape of the garden beyond.

▲ Right at the back of the garden is the fourth 'room' – a play area and fernery.

▼ At night the planters are lit from below with green LED lights, so they appear to hover over the gravel.

▶ Like many city properties the garden lies below the ground floor of the house and these wonderful old steps lead down to it. A cloud-clipped holly is used for sculptural effect beyond the steps.

Surprise

This is a tiny space with a really difficult change of level near to the house and the owners had tried several ways to deal with the rising land but none of them seemed to work. Finally they brought in garden designer, Amanda Patton, who has transformed the garden.

First of all she made sure that there was a usable space at the lower level coming off the sitting room. To make that space the garden had to be pushed back and retaining walls built all around the new sitting area. Left like that there would have been a wall with steps, facing the sitting room, of over a metre. Rather than having that as the daunting view, Amanda has cleverly curved the steps making an invitation to step up into the garden. Placing them as she has, she has also allowed the retaining wall to the left of the steps to be much lower – there's a second smaller wall behind to take the rest of the level change.

The curve in the path also sets up a dynamic which leads you from right to left and back to right again – the journey down this garden is much longer than you would think possible given its small size. At the end of the path is a seat, completely hidden away from the house by tall plants, and that is the second part of the story of this garden.

On top of the strong design, Amanda has planted jungly architectural plants which fill the air with greenery and pretty much completely obscure the boundaries, so the garden's size (or lack of it) is no longer apparent.

Garden Plan

The owners were keen to have a green and lush garden, somewhere they could hide away, so it is mainly formed of deep planted beds.

Structural plants like grasses, bamboos and hostas have been used to get a real jungly feeling.

The boundaries have been unified by horizontal slat trellis work, and they have been nearly hidden by planting as well. The trellis has been painted the same colour as the kitchen units inside the house.

Stepping up the wall to create a raised bed means that plants can be used to soften the surface – without this bed a sheer wall of over a metre high would face the house.

Right at the back a living fence has been put in called a Mobilane screen. It is made from a metal grid covered with plants and can be installed directly into the garden for an instant effect.

By taking the path first to the left and then to the right the journey down the garden has been made as long as possible.

Amanda Patton, the designer, decided to curve the steps around so they lead you up into the garden but don't eat into the upper level too much.

This garden is absolutely tiny, with a change in level of over a metre as the garden rises away from the house.

The bricks match those used on the new extension.

▶ The path through the garden has been formed quite simply using decking circles and slate paddlestones.

▲ At the end of the garden a small seat looks back in towards the rest of the garden.

▶ The strong structure of the garden works well to contain the large specimen plants used.

▲ If you're planning a curved wall in the garden, the curve needs to be quite gentle to make sure the bricks don't stick out – lay out a few bricks on the ground where the curve might be to see how they would form the line.

◀ Even within the tiny garden there are different spaces for people to sit and for a journey down through the garden.

▲ Large plants make great screens so that, at the end of the garden, you really do feel as though you are away from the world.

▶ With a large change in level in a small space, it's difficult to know how to deal with the steps. Put them going straight back into the garden and they'll go almost to the back of the plot. Amanda cleverly curved them round. This is an inviting way to make the steps and allows for the maximum amount of planting on either side.

◀ At one end of the decked area a wooden built-in seat has been painted the same colour as the trellis. It's got bamboos in planters at either side to help soften the wall behind.

White

What do you do if you have a tiny garden? What if your tiny garden is at the front of your house and overlooked on all sides? What if you want a piece of romance in the middle of the town?

This small garden, created by designer Stuart Craine, answers all of these questions. The garden here was enclosed by walls and old hedges and filled with heavy planting and trees. The owners wanted something timeless, elegant and, above all, sheltered from the street scene around. Stuart has taken away the wall and reinstated railings, replaced the old hedge with a beautiful new yew hedge and above this, he has put in pleached limes (trees with tall clear stems and then shaped into a 'hedge' two metres high above the ground) to shelter the garden from the windows of the houses around.

To make the romance Stuart has taken his cue from Sissinghurst Castle in Kent. The garden at Sissinghurst was designed in the 1930s to combine flourishes of planting within a strong architectural structure and it's a great look for a small garden. In winter the architecture of the trees and hedges takes centre stage. In summer the abundance of flowers makes a wonderful contrast to the strong lines around.

Garden Plan

The old, overgrown hedge has been replaced by a new, trim yew hedge which will give year-round seclusion.

Above the hedge, with just a narrow gap for light, are pleached lime trees. These pleached trees have a clear tall stem up to 2m and above that the tree is trained into a flat screen so the whole thing forms a hedge on stilts.

The area isn't big but by tidying up the 'walls' and improving the privacy Stuart has made it a usable sitting area.

Trees as large as this will need staking for several years until they become established. Staking at an angle like this gives more stability than traditional, upright stakes.

On one side is traditional mixed border planting, to give an extra softness to the area.

Stuart has used reclaimed York stone on the ground to create a room within the space for sitting.

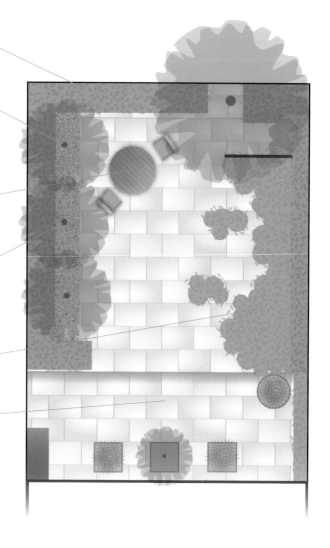

▶ From the outside the garden looks very formal and clipped. It's not until you enter the garden that you see the planted borders.

◀ The garden is inspired by the romantic white border at Sissinghurst, where Vita Sackville-West created an icon of garden design. Like the garden at Sissinghurst this space, although tiny, combines architecture with romance.

▲ Rather than be restricted to just white Stuart has mixed in purples as well.

▲ Pleached trees are perfect to create instant seclusion. To make a wall or fence this high would create issues with planning permission and would also dominate the garden.

▼ The paving is reclaimed York, it is perfect for a cottagey look. Reclaimed materials are very expensive but if the area is small, it's worth looking into.

▲ The garden is a wonderful mix of stylish and traditional. Planting up this classic container with just pure white agapanthus and ivy gives it a modern twist.

◀ Even in a tiny garden like this there's room to store the equipment. A dark painted, low storage box blends back into the garden.

▶ Along one side of the garden Stuart has planted a traditional mixed border. He has beautifully combined leaf shapes and colours.

Circle

This is a wonderful family garden, designed by the owner who isn't a trained garden designer – it is a great example of what you can do with a fairly standard back garden and a little thought.

There were no plans here, the owner didn't measure up, instead he paced it out and marked it out on the ground. What he had a clear grasp of, however, was the need to get a strong shape to the lawn and to create separate rooms off from that central shape.

So the circular lawn holds the entire garden. The retaining wall alongside the patio has been built to its curve, and from it three distinct rooms come off. The large sitting area to the rear is an enclosed and elegant dining area with a table for 10. In the other corner of the garden at the rear is a play area with a slide and climbing frame, and, to the side, is a small area with a table for four which is often in the shade. A hammock swings here for balmy afternoons.

It really is worth thinking through your design and walking it out on the ground. For example if the lawn had come right up to the retaining wall around the patio, it would have been difficult to maintain, so the owner has put in a sweep of chippings with neatly laid out box balls.

But the huge lesson here is to create those shapes within the garden and fill in what's left with planting.

Garden Plan

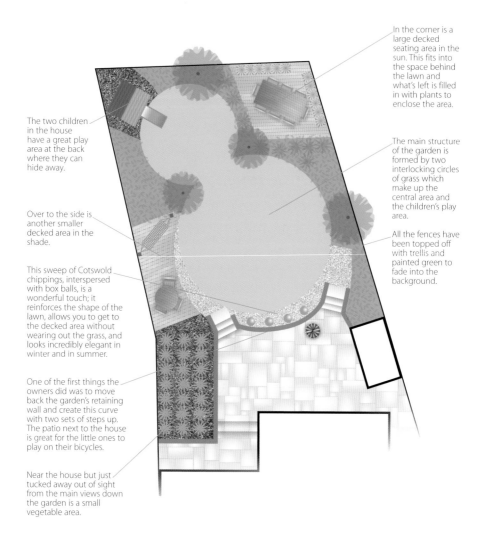

In the corner is a large decked seating area in the sun. This fits into the space behind the lawn and what's left is filled in with plants to enclose the area.

The main structure of the garden is formed by two interlocking circles of grass which make up the central area and the children's play area.

All the fences have been topped off with trellis and painted green to fade into the background.

The two children in the house have a great play area at the back where they can hide away.

Over to the side is another smaller decked area in the shade.

This sweep of Cotswold chippings, interspersed with box balls, is a wonderful touch; it reinforces the shape of the lawn, allows you to get to the decked area without wearing out the grass, and looks incredibly elegant in winter and in summer.

One of the first things the owners did was to move back the garden's retaining wall and create this curve with two sets of steps up. The patio next to the house is great for the little ones to play on their bicycles.

Near the house but just tucked away out of sight from the main views down the garden is a small vegetable area.

▶ The vegetable garden is just the right size for a family of four. By placing it right near the back door the owner has made sure it's easy to keep an eye on and to water if necessary.

9

▲ Strung between two sturdy uprights on the smaller deck is a hammock. Great for adults and children to use.

◀ Around the back of the main sitting area the owner has put in raised wooden containers to hold grasses and climbing plants, to lessen the impact of the high fences behind.

▶ The box balls are surrounded by light-coloured Cotswold chippings. They are large enough not to travel onto the lawn and very light and bright to set off the dark green of the box.

◀ Between the vegetable area and the small sitting area is a woven screen to divide the two off.

▲ When the children's friends come around there's plenty of room at the big table.

▼ The box balls give a wonderful 'implied hedge' between the lawn and the retaining wall. If the lawn went right up to the wall not only would cutting the grass be difficult but it would also be all too easy for children (and adults) to fall over it.

▲ These outdoor canvases are from ingarden.

Amphitheatre

The owners of this garden wanted a place for their family; a garden that was easy to live with but also something modern and stylish. So Charlotte Rowe, the garden's designer, has kept the lawn – that mainstay of family gardens – but added a twist.

The shapes are the first things you notice about the design. Strong and bold squares and oblongs sit alongside the central dipped circular lawn. They don't fit together neatly but work to create different patterns as they draw near each other and pull away. This is assured design – Charlotte is making shapes in the garden which fit together artistically and create interest. By manipulating these shapes she has transformed what could have been standard into something truly contemporary and interesting.

The contrasts don't just come from the shapes in this garden. Textures form huge contrasts with the lightest, brightest and cleanest paving, the limestone, pitted against lawn and gravel.

The styles of different elements in the garden also play off each other. At the one extreme are the old stones from an unwanted rockery, now used to line the amphitheatre, which are full of moss and without a straight line among them. At the other there is the sawn limestone, laid in an exact and regular grid.

Garden Plan

Right next to the house there was a dilemma. The clients intend to extend out but not immediately. It would be pointless to put expensive materials here so Charlotte has extended the gravel right back to the house – it's an easy material to lift when the time comes.

The owners wanted a fish pond and Charlotte has included a beautiful raised pond which together with the elegantly planted beds makes a square. This square plays off the square of limestone to its right and the square defined by limestone in the lawn.

The strong pale lines of limestone reach out into the lawn to give a modern feel to an otherwise traditional layout.

Charlotte has taken control of the shapes of this garden. The most important shape is that of the large lawn, which the clients wanted to keep.

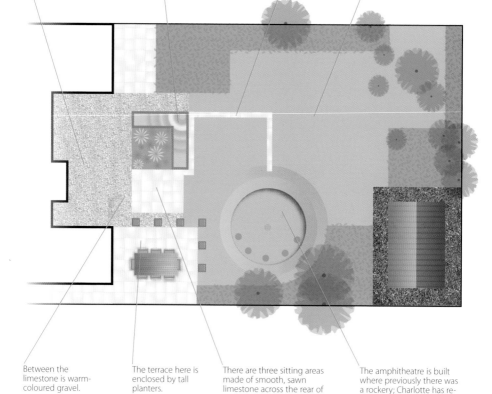

Between the limestone is warm-coloured gravel.

The terrace here is enclosed by tall planters.

There are three sitting areas made of smooth, sawn limestone across the rear of the house to catch the sun at different times of the day.

The amphitheatre is built where previously there was a rockery; Charlotte has re-used the stones from that to create the retaining walls.

▶ The limestone flooring gives a strong white gloss to the areas around the house which set off the containers and the planting perfectly.

▲ Inside the grass amphitheatre, the lawn could have been left bare, but instead there are five box globes and a central stone feature – just right to bring the area alive and give it meaning.

◀ The modern fish pond forms two sides of a square containing pretty Mediterranean and evergreen plants. The materials of the garden work perfectly together, the strong line of white limestone cuts through the lawn to make a modern, artistic statement.

▶ The planting is mixed shrubs, perennials and grasses.

▲ Pleached hornbeam trees have been used to give maximum screening from the neighbours. Pleached trees have a clear stem up to six feet or so and are then trained to make a 'hedge on stilts'.

▲ Tall planters are great for defining different areas of the garden. These, from Iota, are topped with square-cut box bushes.

▲ If you have any old materials, an unwanted wall or an obsolete rockery, look to see if the materials are worth re-using. It saves money, saves the environment and can look stunning.

◄ The amphitheatre is a perfect example of a feature that works for all ages. It's elegant and interesting enough for adults, it's a joy for the younger children in the house and, for the teenagers, a great place to lounge.

▼ The stones from the rockery that was taken away work perfectly to make the retaining walls and create a great mix of old and modern in the garden.

Directory

Products

CED
Natural stone
www.ced.ltd.uk

Crocus
Online plants
www.crocus.co.uk

ingarden
Products for modern outdoor living
www.ingarden.co.uk

Iota
Contemporary pots and planters
www.iotagarden.com

Mobilane
Green screens
www.mobilane.co.uk

The Garden Trellis Company
Trellis and garden woodwork
www.gardentrellis.co.uk

Designers

Acres Wild Garden and Landscape Design
www.acreswild.co.uk

Amanda Patton
www.amandapatton.co.uk

Ann Pearce
Metamorphosis Design
www.metamorphosisdesign.co.uk

Charlotte Rowe Garden Design
www.charlotterowe.com

Debbie Jolley
www.debbiejolleygardendesign.co.uk

George Carter
grcarter@easynet.co.uk

Ian Kitson
Chartered landscape architect and garden designer
www.iankitson.com

Stuart Craine Gardens Ltd
www.stuartcraine.com